Jacob's Hoop

Written By Karen Franco

Illustrated By Jia Jia

JACOB'S HOOP
Copyright © 2014 by Karen Franco

ISBN-13: 978-0692265765
ISBN-10: 0692265767

All Rights Reserved. No parts of this book may be reproduced or utilized in any form or by any means, electronic or mechanical, including photocopying, scanning, recording, or by any information storage and retrieval system known or hereafter invented, without permission, in writing from the publisher.

To contact Karen Franco or to order a copy of this book, please visit www.karenfrancobooks.com

Published by
AMITY Publications
37 Rogers Run
Barrington, NH 03825
www.amitypublications.com

Printed in the United States of America

Acknowledgment

To my husband, Chris...
always supportive, always listening,
and my biggest fan.
Thank you!

Dedicated to...

My son Jacob, my daily inspiration, and to *Every Child's Place*, which was a blessing to our family and is still one for many families today.

Hi, I'm Jacob and I like to play basketball.

I can dribble the ball, do a jump shot, shoot a free throw and even slam dunk.

Well...I try to do all those things,
but just not like all the other kids.

That's why I have Jacob's Hoop.

At *Every Child's Place*, my child care center,
my friends and I play basketball all the time.

Every Child's Place is the best because kids like me are taken care of and loved for who we are. We have fun and are safe and happy.

I always use my favorite red and white basketball.

When we play, I like to say, "He shoots... he scores."
The kids think that's funny so we all laugh.

Sometimes playing basketball can be hard for me.

The hoop is too high and I can't make a basket.

I don't shoot the ball the same as the other kids.

I may run a little slower or stumble when I try to dribble.

I even throw the ball the wrong way when I am trying to shoot a free throw. I get frustrated.

That's why I have Jacob's Hoop.

My friends tell me to keep trying, but no matter how many times I try, I just can't play the way they do.

I get sad and I may cry, but my friends understand.

Ms. Ginny, my teacher, is always there to help me feel better.

She tells me, "Jacob, you are special. I want you to play basketball anyway you want to as long as you have fun."

One day, a big surprise was waiting for me at *Every Child's Place*.

Outside was a new playground with a soft floor and toys just for me and my friends. The best part was a basketball hoop just my size.

On top of the backboard, in big green letters it said, "Jacob's Hoop."

Life brings around happy and sad times, easy and difficult challenges.
All help us be the best we can be.

Thanks to *Every Child's Place*, I have lots of fun playing basketball everyday.

That's because I have Jacob's hoop.

Not the End . . .

www.ingramcontent.com/pod-product-compliance
Lightning Source LLC
Chambersburg PA
CBHW041540040426
42446CB00002B/172